THIS NOTEBOOK

BELONGS TO

NOTEBOOK

NOTEBOOK

NOTEBOOK

NOTEBOOK

NOTEBOOK

NOTEBOOK

NOTEBOOK

NOTEBOOK

NOTEBOOK

NOTEBOOK

NOTEBOOK

NOTEBOOK

NOTEBOOK

NOTEBOOK

NOTEBOOK

NOTEBOOK

NOTEBOOK

NOTEBOOK

NOTEBOOK

NOTEBOOK

NOTEBOOK

NOTEBOOK

NOTEBOOK

NOTEBOOK

NOTEBOOK

NOTEBOOK

NOTEBOOK

NOTEBOOK

NOTEBOOK

NOTEBOOK

NOTEBOOK

NOTEBOOK

NOTEBOOK

NOTEBOOK

NOTEBOOK

NOTEBOOK

NOTEBOOK

NOTEBOOK

NOTEBOOK

NOTEBOOK

NOTEBOOK

NOTEBOOK

NOTEBOOK

NOTEBOOK

NOTEBOOK

NOTEBOOK

NOTEBOOK

NOTEBOOK

NOTEBOOK

NOTEBOOK

NOTEBOOK

NOTEBOOK

NOTEBOOK

NOTEBOOK

NOTEBOOK

NOTEBOOK

NOTEBOOK

NOTEBOOK

NOTEBOOK

NOTEBOOK

NOTEBOOK

NOTEBOOK

NOTEBOOK

NOTEBOOK

NOTEBOOK

NOTEBOOK

NOTEBOOK

NOTEBOOK

NOTEBOOK

NOTEBOOK

NOTEBOOK

NOTEBOOK

NOTEBOOK

NOTEBOOK

NOTEBOOK

NOTEBOOK

NOTEBOOK

NOTEBOOK

NOTEBOOK

NOTEBOOK

NOTEBOOK

NOTEBOOK

NOTEBOOK

NOTEBOOK

www.ingramcontent.com/pod-product-compliance
Lightning Source LLC
Chambersburg PA
CBHW070428220526
45466CB00004B/1577
* 9 7 8 1 6 7 8 4 0 1 7 2 6 *